A. M. ASHIURAKIS

SPOKEN ARABIC
SELF-TAUGHT

DAR AL-FERGIANI
9Al-Dahabi Square, Manshiat Al-Bakri
P.O.Box 2328, Horria, Heliopolis
Cairo, Egypt
Tel.: 2905895

ISBN 1 85077 090 5

Acknowledgement

My thanks to Betty and Nancy for their enthusiasm and help

A. M. ASHIURAKIS

CONTENTS

CONTENTS

PREFACE

This pocket phrase book has been prepared for those who are eager to acquire a working knowledge of every-day spoken Arabic and put it into every-day use.

It is based on different conversational subjects which are mainly intended to assist the reader to understand, step by step, the various forms of construction of phrases and sentences, e.g. what would you say in Arabic if you were going to invite some one? How would you say the time or ask some one to help you? And other practical expressions you would need in the market, at the hotel, at the butcher, etc. in your daily transactions. However, any lesson may be studied in any order you please, but it is necessary that a knowledge of simple rules must firstly be mastered.

Finally, it is recommended that you should never lose any opportunity to use your newly-acquired knowledge of spoken Arabic.

GUIDE TO THE READING OF ARABIC WORDS

English Alphabet	Nearest Equivalent Arabic & Pronunciation	Arabic Alphabet	Arabic Pronunciation
A	Alif as in add	أ	Alif
B	Ba as in bath	ب	Ba
C	Seen as in seen	ت	Ta
D	Dal as in dead	ث	Tha
E	no equivalent	ج	Jim
F	Fe as in fed	ح	Hha
G	Jim as in junk	خ	Kha
H	Ha as in hate	د	Dal
I	no equivalent	ذ	Thal or dhal
J	Jim as in junk	ر	Ra
K	Kaf as in kaftan	ز	Za
L	Lam as in lemon	س	Sin
M	Mim as in melon	ش	Shin
N	Nun as in noon	ص	Sad
O	no equivalent	ض	Dad
P	Ba as in baker	ط	Ta
Q	Kaf as in kaftan	ظ	Tha
R	Raa as in rather	ع	Ain
S	Seen as in sent	غ	Ghain
T	Ta as in take	ف	Fa
U	no equivalent	ق	Qaf or Kaf
V	Fa as in fat	ك	Kef
W	Waw as in wax	ل	Lam
X	no equivalent	م	Mim
Y	Ya as in young	ن	Nun
Z	Zen as in zebra	ﻫ	Ha
		و	Waw
		ى	Ya

ABBREVIATIONS

m	Masculine
f	Feminine
pl	Plural
s	Singular
n	Noun
prep	Preposition
adj	Adjective
v	Verb
pa	Past Tense
pre	Present Tense
imp	Imperative or command
pp	Page
colloq	Colloquial
cl	Classical

A GUIDE TO GRAMMAR

PRONOUNS		POSSESSIVE	
I	**Anna**	My book	**Kitaabi**
We	**Nahnu**	Our book	**Kitaabna**
He	**Huwa**	His book	**Kitaabah**
She	**Heya**	Her book	**Kitaabha**
They	**Henn (f)**	Their book	**Kitaabhenn**
They	**Hum (m)**	Their book	**Kitaabhum**
You	**Anta (m) s.**	Your book	**Kitaabak**
You	**Anti (f) s.**	Your book	**Kitaabik**
You	**Antum (m) pl.**	Your book	**Kitaabkum**
You	**Anten (f) pl.**	Your book	**Kitaabken**

VERB TO BE PRESENT

I am	**Ana**
You are	**Anta (m)**
	Anti (f)
He is	**Huwa**
She is	**Heya**
It is	**Huwa (m)**
	Heya (f)
We are	**Nah-nu**
They are	**Hum (m)**
	Henna (f)

VERB TO BE PAST TENSE

I was	**Kunt**
You were	**Kunt (s) kuntum (pl)**
He ⎫	**Kan**
She ⎬ was	**Kanat**
It ⎭	**Kan (m) kanat (f)**
We were	**Kunna**
They were	**Kanu (m) kanan (f)**

N.B. The Verb To Be in the Present Tense is rarely used in conversation.

VERB TO HAVE

I have	Andi
You have — singular	Andak (m)
	Andik (f)
You have — plural	Andakum (m)
	Andaken (f)
He has	Andahu
She has	Andaha
We have	Andana
They have	Andahum (m)
	Andahen (f)
I had	Kan andi
You had	Kan andak (m)
	Kan andik (f)
We had	Kan andana
They had	Kan andahum (m)
	Kan andahen (f)
She had	Kan andaha
He had	Kan andahu

PRACTICAL RULES TO SPOKEN ARABIC

	Pronouns	Possessive	Noun Suffixes
I	— Anna	My book	= Kitaab I
We	— Nah-nu	Our	= Kitaab Na
He	— Huwa	His	= Kitaab Ah
She	— Heya	Her	= Kitaab Ha
They	— Henna (f)	Their	= Kitaab Henn
They	— Hum (m)	Their	= Kitaab Hum
You	— Anta (m) s.	Your	= Kitaab Ak
You	— Anti (f) s.	Your	= Kitaab Ik
You	— Antum (m) pl.	Your	= Kitaab Kum
You	— Anten (f) pl.	Your	= Kitaab Ken

OBJECTIVE PRONOUNS

			Suffixes
Me	— Call = (Naadi)	Call Me	Naadi Ni
Us	—	Call Us	Naadi Na
Him	—	Call Him	Naadi H
Her	—	Call Her	Naadi Ha
Them	— (f)	Call Them	Naadi Hen
Them	— (m)	Call Them	Naadi Hum
You	— (m) s. (Onaadi)	I Call You	Naadi Ka
You	— (f) s.	I Call You	Naadi Ki
You	— (m) pl.	I Call You	Naadi Kum
You	— (f) pl.	I Call You	Naadi Ken

DEMONSTRATIVES

This	— Hatha (m)	Hathi-hi (f)
That	— Hathak (m)	Hathik (f)
These	— Hathom (m)	Hathein (f)
Those	— Hathok (m)	Hathikahen (f)

PLURALS

The suffix (In) is for all male } Regular Nouns
The suffix (At) is for all Female

A Teacher (m) **Mudarris** Teachers **Mudarris (In)**

A Woman Teacher (f)   Women Teachers
   Mudarrisa   **Mudarris (At)**

Irregular nouns are formed by an internal change and they must be memorised e.g.

Pen (s) **Galam (s) Ag-laam (pl)**
Window (s) **Shubbak**

Man (s) men **Rajel (s) Rajaala (pl)**
Monkey (s) **Gherd (s) Ghorood (pl)**
Door (s) **Baab (s) Be-baan (pl)**

N.B. The Particle **(EIN)** is placed after a noun to mean duality e.g.

A book **Kitaab**
Two books **Kitabein**
A chair **Kursi**
Two chairs **Kursiein**
A table **Taw-la**
Two tables **Taw-Itein**

NOUNS AND ADJECTIVES

Nouns and adjectives can be made feminine by suffixing the
letter (a) for the singular and (at) for the plural.

COMPARISONS

More than	Ak-thar min
Less than	Aqal min
Good	Hasàn
Better	Ah-san
Bad	Radee
Worse	Ar-da
The best	Al-ah-san
The worst	Al-ar-da

ADVERBS

Well	Hasàn
Badly	Ala nah-oo radee
Quietly	Be-hudoo
Always	Day-man
Sometimes	Ah-yaanan
Usually	Adatan
For the time being	Fee al-wagt al-haadar
By chance	Be-assod-fà
Only	Bass or Faqat
Openly	Be-saraaha
Seldom	Naa-diran

INTERROGATIVE

Interrogative sentences are generally made by either a tone of voice or the word **Hal** as a prefix. e.g.

Do you know the way? **Ta-ref attareegh?** or
Hal-ta-ref attareegh?

Have you a pencil? **Andak galam?**
Hal-andak galam?

Conjugation of Verb	"To Drink" Past Tense	Verb Suffixes
I drank	Sharabt	... T
We drank	Sharabna	... NA
He drank	Sharaba	... A
She drank	Sharabat	... T
They (m) drank	Sharabu	... U
They (f) drank	Sharaban	... AN
You (m/s) drank	Sharabt	... T
You (f/s) drank	Sharabti	... TI
You (m/pl) drank	Sharabatu	... TU
You (f/pl) drank	Sharabtan	... AN

Conjugation of Verb	"To Drink" Present Tense	Verb Prefixes
I drink	Nashrab	NA ...
We drink	Nashrabu	NA ... U
He drinks	Yashrab	YE or YA ...
She drinks	Tashrab	TA ...
They drink (m)	Yashrabu	YE or YA ... U
They drink (f)	Yashraban	YE or YA ... AN
You drink (m)	Tashrab	TA ...
You drink (m/pl)	Tashrabu	TA ... U
You drink (f)	Tashrabi	TA ... I
You drink (f/pl)	Tashraban	TA ... AN

VERBS

Note how the following tenses are formed in the spoken vernacular.

1. Present Simple Tense   **Al-haather**
   I drink water everyday.   **Nash-rab emmoyaa kul-youm.**

   I go to the office.   **Nem-shi ila al-mak-tab.**
   She reads the lesson.   **Tagh-ra addars.**

2. Past Simple Tense   **Al-maathee**
   I drank water yesterday.   **Sharabt emmoyaa ams.**
   I went to the office.   **Meshait ila al-maktab.**
   Last night   **El-bareh bee-alleil**
   She read the lesson.   **Gharat addars.**

3. Future Simple Tense   **Al-mustaq-bl**
   I shall drink tea.   **Sa-nash-rab shaahe.**
   Tomorrow   **Bukra** or **Ghadan**
   I shall go to Spain.   **Sa-nemshi ila esbaaniya.**
   Next week   **Al-Isboo ajjaee**
   She will read.   **Sa-tagh-ra.**
   The book after   **Al-kitaab ba-ad**
   This lesson   **Hatha addars**

4. Present Continuous Tense   **Al-mudaara al-mustamer**

   I am drinking water now.   **Nash-rab fee emmoyaa tawwa.**

   (or)   **(Ghaad) nash-rab fee**

   (The prefix **(Ghaad)** can
   be dropped)

   I am going to the office.   **emmoyaa tawwa**
                                        Maashi ila al-maktab.

5. Past Continuous Tense	**Al-mathee al-mustamer**
I was drinking tea as Ali came in the room.	**Kunt nash-rab fee Ashaahe andama dakhala Ali fee al-huj-ra.**

SUMMARY

The stem of the Verb in the Arabic language is the Past Tense of the 3rd person masculine singular e.g.

To drink	**Sharaba**	He drank	**Sharaba**
To go out	**Kharaja**	He went	**Kharaja**
To speak	**Takallama**	He spoke	**Takallama**
To walk	**Mashaa**	He walked	**Mashaa**
To write	**Kataba**	He wrote	**Kataba**

N.B. At the end of each Verb there is the letter **(A)** as a suffix to the Past Tense of the 3rd person masculine singular. This letter can be dropped at the time of speaking.

6. The imperative. (To Command).
   Some letters prefixed to the Verb in the present Tense.

Drink	**(A) Shrab (m/s)**	**Ashrabi (f/s)**
Bring	**Jeeb (m/s)**	**Jeebi (f/s)**
Write	**Ak-tubu (m/pl)**	**Ak-tban (f/pl)**
Abandon	**At-rek (m)**	**At-reki (f)**
Break	**Ak-ser (m)**	**Ak-seri (f)**

You have noted in the previous pages how the verbs in the past and in the present tenses were conjugated by suffixes and prefixes. These should be studied in order to apply them to other required verbs.

	Past Tense	Present	Command
To leave	Taraka	Yet-rek	At-rek
To change	Baddala	Yebaddel	Baddil
To look for	Dawwar	Yeddawer	Dawwer
To smoke	Dakh-khan	Yedakh-khen	Dakh-khin
To speak	Takallam	Yetakallam	Takallam
To learn	Ta-allam	Yata-allem	Ta-allem
To come	Jaa	Eejee	Ta-aal
To walk	Masha	Yemshi	Imshi
To give	Atà	Ya-tee	A'-tee
To read	Ghara	Yegh-ra	Agh-ra
To sell	Ba'ah	Yabee	Beea
To bring	Jaab	Yijeeb	Jeeb
To drive	Saagh	Yisoogh	Soogh
To go	Masha	Yemshi	Imshi
To see	Shaaf	Yishoof	Shoof
To rest	Staraah	Yestareeh	Istareeh
To clean	Naddafa	Yenaddaf	Naddif

	Past Tense	Present	Command
Can	Gh-dar	Yagh-dar	—
Must	—	Yajib	—
To take	Akhada	Yakhud	Khud
To use	As-tamala	Yestamel	Istamel
To tell	Ghaal	Yeghool	Ghool
To lock	Sakkar	Yessaker	Sakker

	Past Tense	Present	Command
To say	Ghaal	Yeghool	Ghool
To wash	Ghasal	Yegh-sel	Igh-sil
To ask	Sa-al	Yes-al	Is-al
To carry	Hamal	Yeh-mal	Ih-mal
To carry	Shaal	Yesheel	Sheel
To show	Warra	Yewarri	Warri
To call	Naada	Yenaadi	Naadi
To put	Hatta	Ye-hett	Hett
To sweep	Kanasa	Yek-nis	Ik-nis
To under-stand	Fahama	Yef-ham	If-ham
To want	Araada	Yi-reed	—
To hear	Samaà	Yas-maa	Is-maa
To explain	Fahama	Yef-ham	If-ham
To know	Arafa	Ya-ref	A-ref
To try	Jaraba	Ye-jarab	Ja-reb
To like	Habba	Yi-hibb	Hibb
	Past Tense	**Present**	**Command**
To think	Fakkara	Ye-fakker	Fakker
To open	Fataha	Yaf-tah	Af-tah
To teach	Allama	Ye-allam	Allim
To ride	Rakiba	Yar-kib	Ar-kib
To send	Arsala	Yer-sil	Ar-sil
To shut	Qafala	Yaq-fil	Iq-fil
To sit	Jalasa	Yaj-lis	Ij-lis
To stand	Waqafa	Ya-qif	Qif
To wear	Labasa	Yal-bes	Al-bis
To inform	Balagha	Yeballegh	Balligh
To forget	Nasà	Yansà	Ansa

To throw	Ramaa	Yar-me	Ar-me
To arrive	Wasala	Yasell	—
To repair	Sallaha	Yasallah	Sallah
To cook	Tabbakha	Yatabbakh	At-bekh

AUXILIARY VERBS

(INTERROGATIVE AND NEGATIVE)

The following English auxiliary Verbs:
can, could, shall, should, will, would, do, does, did, must, may, might, ought to, be, am, is, was, are, were, has, have and had. When they are in the interrogative form, use the word (**HAL**) and in the negative form use these two words **MA. . . & . . . SH** e.g.

Can you drink tea?	**Hal-tagh-dar tash-rab shaahe?**
Yes, I can.	**Ai-wa nagh-dar.**
No, I can't.	**La, ma-nagh-dar-sh.**
I must go to school.	**Yajib nemshi ila al-mad-rasa.**
Must I go to school?	**Hal-yajib nemshi ila al-mad-rasa?**
Yes, you must.	**Ai-wa yajib.**
No, you must'nt.	**La ma-yajib-sh.**
I shall write to-morrow.	**Sa-aktub bukra.**
Shall I write to-morrow?	**Hal-sa-aktub bukra?**
Yes, you will write.	**Ai-wa sa-taktub.**
No, you will not.	**La ma-tik-tib-sh.**
Do you have lunch?	**Hal-andak ghadaa?**
Yes, I have.	**Ai-wa andee.**
No, I haven't.	**La ma-andee-sh.**

Were there many people in the house?	Hal kaan hunaak naas katherin fee al-beit?
Yes, there were some.	Ay-wa kaan fee ba-ath.
No, there weren't any.	La ma-kaan-sh fee had.
Are you enjoying yourself?	Hal-enta mutamateea binaf-sak?
Yes, I am.	Ay-wa mutamateea.
No, I am not.	La-manish-mutamateea.
Will you come again in my department?	Hal-tureed it-jee marra Taanya fee idaarati?
Yes, I hope, I will.	Ay-wa aamal enjee.
No, I shall not.	La man-jee-sh.
Could you come later?	Hal tas-tatee it-jee baadein?
Yes, I can.	Ay-wa nastatee.
No, I cannot.	La ma-nastatee-sh.
Have you made a mistake?	Hal-akh-ta-at?
Yes, I made.	Ay-wa akh-ta-at.
No, I did not.	La ma-akh-ta-ti-sh.

(1) The word (**GHA-AD**) is a helping particle used with Verb To Be (**kANA**) to express continuous tense e.g.:

I am writing	**Ana gha-ad naktib**
A letter	**fee resaala**
I was writing	**Ana kunt naktib**
A letter	**fee resaala**
I had been writing	**Ana kunt gha-ad naktib**
A letter	**fee resaala**

23

(2) Each of the following auxiliary verbs is generally used in colloquial arabic to denote future tense:

Youreed = Want (or)
= Wish e.g.:

We will see him to morrow	**Nah-na nurid enshofoh buckra**
I will go to London to morrow	**Ana urid amshi lee-lundan buckra**

(3) The word "AL-AN" meaning "NOW" is also used as a helping particle to denote near future e.g.:

I am coming	**Al-an en-jee**
He is leaving	**Al-an yemshi**

24

RELATIVE PRONOUNS

Who — whom — that	Illi
When (time)	Kaif (or) endama
Where (place)	Illi ... fee (or) haithu
While (time)	Lamma
How	Kaif
Who ... ?	Man ... ?
Whom ... ?	Man ... ?
Whose ... ?	Lee-man (or) emta'man ?
Which ... ?	Ay-en ... ?
What ... ?	Maatha
When ... ?	Mata ... ?
Where ... ?	Wain ... ? (or) menain ... ?
Why ... ?	Laysh ... ? (or) leemaatha ... ?
How ... ?	Kaif ... ?
How many ... ?	Kam (or) gheddash ... ?
How much ... ?	Beish (or) bekam ... ?
How long ... ?	Kam ... ?
How far ... ? etc.	Kam ... ?

HOW TO FRAME QUESTIONS

Who is that man?	**Man hathak arrajel?**
Whom you met today?	**Man qaabalt al-youm?**
Whose book is this?	**Leemann hatha al-kitaab?**
Which is the best car?	**Ay ah-san sayyara?**
What is this?	**Shinu hatha?**
When can I see you?	**Amta nagh-dar enshoofak?**
Where can I buy this?	**Fein (or) Wain nagh-dar nesh-teri hatha?**
Why are you late?	**Leemaatha (or) Laysh anta muta-akher?**
How do you say this in Arabic?	**Kaif t-ghool hatha bil-arabee?**
Where do you come from?	**Min-ain anta jaaee?**
Who — whom — that (Relative Pronoun)	**Illi (for all m.f.s. & pl)**
The man (who) wrote the letter is my father.	**Arrajil (illi katab arrisaala huwa abee.**
The garden which is at the back of the house is not mine.	**Al-hadeeqa illi khalf al-bait mush lee.**
The man whom you spoke to in the street is my friend.	**Arrajil illi takallamt ma-ahu fee ashaaree huwa sadeeqi.**
The flowers that my friend gave me have died.	**Annuwaar illi ataahum lee sadeeqi maatoo.**
This is the lady whose dress you have.	**Hathi heya assayeda illi fustan-ha andak. (m)**
When	**Kaif** (slang) (or) **endama** (ci)
Come when you are free	**Taal kaif mat-koonish mash-ghool**
(or)	**Taal endama takoon Ghair mash-ghool**

Where	Illi . . . fee . . . (or) haithu (cl)
That is the office where	Hathaak huwa al-maktab
I was yesterday	Illi koont fee ams
While (in the time that)	Lamma
He said nothing while	Huwa ma-ghaalish ai-shay
I was speaking	Lamma koont atakallam
Who — whom — that	Illi
We saw the people	Nah-nu shefna annaas
Who were working in the house.	Illi kaanu yash-taghulu Fee al-manzil.
The man whom you met is	Arrajil illi qaabalta
The director	Huwa al-moodeer
How	Kaif
Tell me how you wrote the letter.	Ghool-li kaif katabt arrisaala.

REFLEXIVE PRONOUNS

I did it myself.

Can you cook for yourself?

I hurt myself.

She herself bought the bread.

He cut himself.

Did you see how he cut himself?

You yourself said so.

Ask yourself what do you want.

We ourselves will write the letter.

The workers themselves have said so.

Amal-tahu be-nafsi.

Hal-tagh-dar tat-bakh be-nafsak?

Jarah-t nafsi.

Heya be-nafsiha ish-tarat al-khubza.

Huwa jarah nafsah.

Hal-shuft (ra-ait) kaif jarah nafsah?

Anta be-nafsak ghult (or) hekky.

As-al nafsak maatha tureed.

Nah-nu be-nafsina sa-naktub arrisaala.

Al-ummaal be-nafsihum ghaloo hakatha.

GREETINGS

Peace be upon you	**Assalaam alay-kum**
In reply	**Wa alay-kum assalaam**
Good morning	**Sabah-al-khair**
Good evening	**M'sà-al'khair**
Good night	**Amsà-ala-khair (m)**
	Amsì-ala-khair (f)
Good night everyone	**Amsoo-ala-khair (pl)**
Hello!	**Ahlan-wa-sah-lan**
How are you?	**Kaif-halak (m)**
	Kaif-halik (f)
I am well	**Taib (m) Taiba (f)**
. . . thank-you	**Shukran**
Not at all	**Af-wan**
Will you please?	**Min-fadlak (m)**
	Min-fadlik (f)
How do you do?	**Fursa-saeeda (or)**
	Ahlan-wa-sah-lan
Yes	**Na-am (cl)**
	Ay-wa (slang)
This is a . . .	**Hatha (m)**
	Hathi-hi (f)
You are welcome	**Ahlan-wa-sah-lan**
What is the matter?	**La-baas (or) Shinu-fee**
Good	**Kuwais (m)**
	Kuwaisa (f)
Bad	**Mush kuwais (m)**
	Mush kuwaisa (f)
Good gracious (oh dear)	**Ya salaam!**
Cheer up!	**Af-rah**
Never mind	**Ma-aleish**

USEFUL EXPRESSIONS

What is your name?	**Shinu asmak (m)** **Shinu asmik (f)**
Please	**Min-fadlak (m)** **Min-fadlik (f)**
Please sit down.	**Tafadal ejles. (m)** **Tafadli ejlesi. (f)**
May I see you?	**Mumkin enshoofak (m)** **Mumkin enshoofik (f)**
Of course, please do.	**Tab-ann-tafathal.**
Thank you	**Shukran**
Do not mention it.	**Af-wan.**
What is the matter?	**La-baas (or) Shinu-fee?**
Nothing.	**La-shai (or) Ma-feeshai.**
Where have you been?	**When kent (m)?** **When kunti (f)?**
Please come here.	**Min-fathlak ta-aal hana.**
Please go there.	**Min-fathlak emshi hanaak.**
This is good.	**Hada kuwais (m).** **Hadi kuwaisa (f).**
I think so.	**Youmken (or) Mumkin.**
I do not think so.	**Mush mumken.**
You are right.	**Andak hagh.**
Very well	**Ta'yeb (or) Kuwais**
Give my regards to . . .	**Balligh salaami ila . . .**
By chance	**Be-assood-fa**
I don't care a bit.	**La yaḥummuni abadan.**

Allow me	Asmah-li (m)
I am very sorry.	Muta-assef jiddan.
Don't worry.	La tash-ghool baalak. (m)
Congratulations.	Mab-rook.
Cheers!	Fee sahattak! (m)
Allow me to introduce ...	Asmah-li oorefak
... you to Mr.	Bissayed ...
Just a minute	Lah-tha minfath-lak
Pleased to see you.	Forsa-saeeda.
How are you feeling now?	Kaif sah-ttak tawa? (m)
	Kaif sah-ttik tawa? (f)
Happy birthday	Eed-meelaad saeed
Happy feast	Eed-saeed
Happy anniversary	Kul-sana wa-anta ta'yeb (m)
The same to you	Shukran
By all means	Ya-salaam tafaddal
Certainly	Tab-an
It's a fine day.	Nahaar kuwais.
Today	Al-youm
It is dusty today.	Ajaaj al-youm
It is cold today.	Bard al-youm.
It is hot.	Haarr (hamoo) (colloq.)
It is windy.	Reeh-waajid (colloq.).
It is rainy.	Fee-matar al-youm.
It is very cold.	Bar-d shadeed.

GENERAL EXPRESSIONS (2)

Write your name.	**Iktib asmak. (m)** **Iktibi asmik. (f)**
Make tea.	**Deer shahee. (m)**.
Make coffee.	**Deeri ghah-wa. (f)**.
Switch off the light.	**Tafee a-nnoor. (m)**.
Put on the light.	**Walla-ee a-nnoor. (f)**. **Walla a-nnoor. (f)**
Turn off the radio	**Tafee a-rradiu. (m)**
What is this?	**Shinu hatha? (m)**
How old are you?	**Kam umrak? (m)** **Kum umrik? (f)**
How much is this?	**Bikam hatha? (m)**
What have you got?	**Maatha andak? (m)**
Do you know the way?	**Ta-ref attareegh? (m)**
Show me the street.	**Warreeni asharea. (m)**
Do you live here?	**Hal-teskun hana? (m)**
Can I help you?	**Hal-mumken ensaadak?** **(m)**
This is my house.	**Hatha beity. (or) Man-zali.**
I live here.	**Ana nas-kun hana.**
Do you mind if I sit down?	**Hai-tass-mahli naghud** **al-kursi?**
It is impossible.	**La-youmken.**
It is not possible.	**Mush mumken.**
Please yourself.	**Anta wa shaanak (m)**.
As you like	**Keif ma tahib (or) T-reed.**
There is a great difference.	**Fee far-gh kabeer**.
Between them	**Ma bayn-hum**
For (because)	**Ala shaan**

32

GENERAL EXPRESSIONS (3)

That's it.	Kuwais (or) Baahee.
It is too much.	Waajid (or) Katheer.
Come in.	Ta-aal (or) Ud-khal.
I do not know.	Ma-na-refish.
Where are you going?	Wain maashi? (m)
	Wain maashiya? (f)
Come quickly.	Taal-bisur-aa. (m)
	Taali-bisur-aa. (f)
I do not understand you.	Ma-naf-hamsh eish taghool.
What do you want?	Maatha tureed? (m)
I believe so.	Ata-qid hakada.
Do you speak English?	Ta-ref inghileesi?
Speak slowly.	Ta-kalem bish-waish.
I listen to you.	Ana an-sut ilaik. (m)
I am hearing you.	Ana as-maa-feek. (m)
I am ready.	Ana jaahiz.
I have no time.	Ma-andish waqt.
Behind time	Muta-akher
A bit at a time	Qaleelan qaleelan
There is some tea.	Fee esh-waya shaahi.
In the kitchen	Fee al-mat-bakh
But there isn't any milk.	Wa-laakin ma-feesh ay (or) wala haleeb.

INVITATION

Come and visit me at home.	**Ta-aal** (or) **Tafathal zoor-ni fee al-beit.**
When?	**Amta?**
Any time you like.	**Fee ay waqt t-heeb** (or) **Tureed.**
Then I'll come to see you in the afternoon.	**Emmala enjee enshoofak ba-ad ath-hur.**
Is that alright?	**Hal anta mu-wafaq?**
Of course.	**Tab-ann.** (or) **Aywa.**
Splendid (great)	**Atheem**
Have you got a car?	**Hal andak sayyara?**
No, sorry.	**La aasef.**
But that isn't a problem.	**Walakin hathi mush mush-kila.**
I'll get my friend's car.	**Sa-na-khuth sayyarat sadeeqi.**
Agreed, I'll see you next Friday.	**Attafaq-na sa-antatharak youm ajjuma al-muq-bila.**
I hope.	**En-sha-allah.**
Don't forget the appointment.	**Ma-tan-saash al-maw-ed.**
I hope not.	**En-sha allah là.**
Good bye.	**Maa-assalaama.** (or) **Bi-assalaama.**

DAYS OF THE WEEK

Friday	**Al-jum-aa**
Saturday	**As-sabt**
Sunday	**Al-a-had**
Monday	**Al-et-nain**
Tuesday	**At-talaat**
Wednesday	**Al-erbiha**
Thursday	**Al-khamees**

THE ISLAMIC CALENDAR

The Arab months contain 29 and 30 days, but the Islamic year is only 354 days, eleven days less than the Gregorian year. The names of the Muslim months are:

1 Muharram	30 days
2 Safar	29 days
3 Rabi-al-awal	29 days
4 Rabi Ataani	29 days
5 Jumad Al-awal	29 days
6 Jumad A-taani	29 days
7 Rajab	29 days
8 Shaaban	30 days
9 Ramadan	30 days
10 Shawal	30 days
11 Du-al-qada	30 days
12 Du-al-hijja	30 days

MONTHS OF THE YEAR

January	**Yennayer**
February	**Feb-rayer**
March	**Maars**
April	**Ab-reel**
May	**Maayou**
June	**Youniyou**
July	**Youliyou**
August	**Aghusts**
September	**Seb-tember**
October	**Ok-toober**
November	**Noovember**
December	**Deecember**
What is the date to day?	**Shinu attarikh al-youm?**
What month?	**Ai sha-harr? (or) Fe-ay sha-harr?**
It is June (etc.)	**Sha-harr youniyou?**
We are having a party next month.	**Andana haf-la asha-har ajjaee.**

36

NUMERALS

0 Sifr
1 Wahed
2 Et-nain
3 Ta-laat
4 Ar-baa
5 Khamsa
6 Sitta
7 Sab-aa
8 Tamanya
9 Tis-aa
10 Ash-raa
11 Eh-daash
12 At-naash
13 T'lataash
14 Ar-bataash
15 Khams-taash
16 Sitta-sh
17 Saba-tash
18 T'man-tash
19 T'ssa-tash
20 Esh-reen
21 Wahad wa esh-reen
22 Et-nain wa esh-reen

23 T'laata wa esh-reen
24 Ar-baa wa esh-reen
25 Khamsa wa esh-reen
26 Sitta wa esh-reen
27 Sab-aa wa esh-reen
28 T'manya wa esh-reen
29 Tis-aa wa esh-reen
30 Talaateen
40 Ar-ba-een
50 Khamseen
60 Sitteen
70 Sab-een
80 T'maneen
90 T'ss-een
100 Meeya
101 Meeya wa-wahad
102 Meeya wa et'nain
110 Meeya wa ashra
199 Meeya wa t'ssa wa
 t'seen
200 Mee-tain
300 Talat-meeya
900 T'ssa-meeya
1000 Alf
2000 Alfain
1,000,000 Malyoun
2,000,000 Mal-younain
3,000,000 Talaat malayeen

ORDINAL NUMBERS

First	**Al-awal**
Second	**Attaani**
Third	**Attalet**
Fourth	**Arraaba**
Fifth	**Al-khaams**
Sixth	**Assaadis**
Seventh	**Assaabaa**
Eighth	**Attaamen**
Ninth	**Attaasaa**
Tenth	**Al-aashir**
Once	**Marra waheda**
Twice	**Marratain**
Three times	**T'laat marraat**
Four times	**Arbaa marraat**
Quarter	**Rooba**
Half	**Nesf**
Three-quarters	**T'laat ar'baa**
One-third	**Tilt** (or) **Thilth**
Two-thirds	**Tiltain** or *Thilthain*
Minute	**Daqeeqa**
Second	**Thanya**
Hour	**Saa-a**

THE CARDINAL POINTS

East	Sharq
West	Gharb
North	Shamaal (or) Bahri
South	Jenoob (or) Kibli
We went to the east	Mashaina ila ash-sharq
They come from the west	jaa-oo min al-gharb
He comes from the north	jaa-ee min ash-shamaal
Fezzan is in the south	Fazzaan fee ajenoob

THE COLOURS

Colour (s)	Loan (S) al-waan (pl)
White	Ab-yath
Black	As-wad
Green	Akh-dar (or) Akh-thar
Red	Ah-marr
Yellow	As-far
Brown	As-mar
Gray	Ra-maddi
Blue	Az-ragh
Violet	Banaf-saji

CURRENCY

L.E.	1	Gineh
L.E	2	Gineheen
L.E.	3	Talaat Gineh
L.E.	4	Arab-a Gineh
L.E.	5	Khamsa Gineh
L.E.	6	Sitta Gineh
L.E.	7	Sab-a Gineh
L.E.	8	Tamaanya Gineh
L.E.	9	Tissa Gineh
L.E.	10	Ashra Gineh
Quarter Pound		Ruba Gineh
Half Pound		Nesf Gineh

One Egyptian Pound is made up of 100 Piasters

TIME (1)

What time is it?	Kam assa-a?
It is one o'clock	Assa-a waheda
Two	Et-nein
Three	T'laata
Four	Ar-baa
Five	Khamsa
Six	Sitta
Seven	Sab-aa
Eight	T'manya
Nine	T'ssa-aa
Ten	Ash-raa
Eleven	Eh-daash
Twelve	At-naash
Five past one	Wahed wa khamsa
Ten past one	Wahed wa ash-raa
Quarter past one	Wahed wa rooba
Half past one	Wahed wa nesf
Twenty to two	Et-nein illa esh-reen
Quarter to two	Et-nein illa rooba
Ten to two	Et-nein illa ash-raa
Five to two	Et-nein illa khamsa

TIME EXPRESSIONS (2)

Come early tomorrow.	Ta-aal back-ri buk-raa (or) Ghod'wa
Do not come late.	Mat-jish-muta-akhir.
I want to see you.	Enreed enshoofak.
Within	Khilaal (or) Dakhil
After	Ba-ad
Two weeks (a fortnight)	Es-boo-ain
You are one hour late.	Enta lak sa-aa muta-akhir.
It was cold last week.	Kan fee bard fee al-usboo al-maadi, (or) Al-faayet.
My watch is slow.	Saa-ati muta-akhira.
Your watch is fast.	Saa-atak muta-qaddima.
What time is it?	Saa-kam?
Dinner	Tataghadda (v) Ghadà (n)
Dinner?	Tata-ashaa (v) Ashaa (n)
Breakfast	Tef-tar (v) Futoor (n)
Sometimes	Ah-yaanan (or) Baad-al-waqt
At least once	Alal-laqal marraa
As soon as . . .	Haalama . . .
I finish my work	Entahee min shugh-lee
Help yourself	Ta-fadal (or) Tafathal
From . . . to . . .	Min . . . ila . . .
At four o'clock	Anda assaa-a ar-baa

TIME EXPRESSIONS (3)

Today is a holiday.	Al-youm ot-laa.
Tomorrow is not a holiday.	Bu-kra mush at-laa.
Yesterday was a good day.	Ams kaan nahaar kuwais.
The day before yesterday . . .	Awel-ams
. . . I was in Sabratha	Ana-kunt fee sabrata
After tomorrow	Ba-ad buk-ra
I shall see you.	En-shoofak. (m)
Every other day	Youm ba-ad youm
Every day	Kul-youm
Every week	Kul-es-boo
Every month	Kul-sha-har
Every year	Kul-sana
Morning	Sabaah
Noon	Thuher (or) Nesf-nahaar
Mid-day — midnight	Nesf-nahaar — Nesf-allail
Before noon	Gabl athuher
Afternoon	Ba-ad athu-her
Always	Day-man
Early in the morning	Bad-ri fee assabaah
Late	Muta-akhir
Never	Abadan
Now	Al-aan (or) Tawa

SHOPPING

How much is this?	**Bikam hada?** (or) **Hatha?**
Is this for sale?	**Hal-hatha lel-bea?**
Yes, it is.	**Ay-wa.**
No, it is not.	**La, mush lel-bea.**
How much a kilo?	**Baish el-kilo?**
How much a litre?	**Baish-el-litra?**
Expensive, dear	**Ghaali**
Cheap, low price	**Rakhees** (or) **Mush-ghaali**
The shop	**Addukaan** (or) **Al-matjar**
The customer	**Azzuboon** (m)
	Azzuboona (f)
I want half a kilo of . . .	**Enreed nasf kilo min . . .**
Quarter of . . .	**Enreed ruba kilo min . . .**
Give me	**Ateeni**
Send this to . . .	**Ersil hatha ila . . .**
Change (alter) this	**Ghayyer hatha**
Change (exchange)	**Sarref**
Greengrocer	**Khathaar**
Butcher	**Jazzaar**
Baker	**Khabbaaz**
Grocer	**Baggaal**
Fishmonger	**Hawaat** (or) **Baaya samak**

AT THE GROCER'S

Butter	Zubda
Egg (S)	Baitha (s)
Salt	Melah
Pepper	Filfill
Sugar	Sukker (or) Succar
Tea	Shahee
Coffee	Ghah-wa
Rice	Rezz
Macaroni	Macaroona
Tin of Tomatoes	Ulba-tamaatem
Honey	Asall
Biscuits	Bash-koot
Marmalade	Ma'joon (or) Murabba
Cheese	Jub-na
Soap	Saboon
Oil	Zait
Olive	Zaitoon
Vinegar	Khall
Milk	Haleeb
Beans	Fassooliya
Broad beans	Fool
Peas	Bezilya
Lentils	Adass
Flour	Daqeeq (or) Taheen

AT THE BUTCHER'S

Lamb	**Kharoof**
Meat	**La-ham**
Veal or Beef	**Laham bagaar** (or) **Ea-jel**
Mince meat (ground beef)	**Laham maf-room**
Lamb chops or cutlets	**Laham kharoof**
Fillet steak	**Shareehat laham baqar**
Leg of lamb	**Fakh-that-kharoof**
Liver of beef	**Kabdat baqar**
Liver of lamb	**Kabdat kharoof**
Kidney	**Kilwa (s) kilaawi (pl)**
Chicken	**Dajaaja (s) Dajaaj (pl)**

AT THE GREENGROCER'S

Okra	**Baamya**
Onions	**Basal**
Green onions	**Basal khathar**
Dried onions	**Basal yaabis**
Cauliflower	**K-ramb** (or) **Kar-nabeet**
Cucumber	**Kheeyaar**
Peas	**Bezilya**
Beans (green)	**Fasoolya khath-ra**
Tomatoes	**Tamaatem**
Carrots	**Jazer**
Lettuce	**Khass** (or) **Salaata**
Turnips	**Lift**
Egg Plant	**Badenjaan**
Garlic	**Thoom** (or) **Toom**
Radish	**Fajal**
Parsley	**Maa-danoos**

46

Potatoes	**Bataats**
Oranges	**Al-burtu-ghaal**
Apples	**Attufah**
Bananas	**Al-banaani** (or) **Mouz**
Lemons	**Al-limoon**
Apricots	**Mish-mish**
Peaches	**Al-khookh**
Grapes	**Al-anab**
Pears	**Al-kometra**
Figs	**Al-teen**
Water melon	**Batteekh**
Melon	**Batteekh**
Dates	**Tamar or Balah**
Nuts	**Louz**
Chestnuts	**Ghastal** (or) **Gastal**
Pomegranates	**Rommaana (s) Rommaan (pl)**
Almonds	**Louz**
Strawberries	**Faraw-lah**
Fruit(s)	**Faakiha (s) Fawaakih (pl)**

AT THE BAKER'S

Fresh Bread   Eish
Loaf of Bread   Reglfeish

AT THE FISHMONGER'S

Fish	**Samak**
A fish	**Samaka**
Dogfish	**Kalb-bahar**
Salmon	**Salamoon**
Tuna	**Tenn**
Swordfish	**Ib-ra**
Sardines	**Sar-deena**
Pagellus	**Man-koos**
Boops salpa	**Shelba**
Epinephelus	**Al-farooj**
Mugil	**Al-boori**
Mullet	**At-treelya**
Fresh	**Taa-za**
Not fresh	**Mush-taa-za**

AT THE HOTEL

My name is . . .	Asmi . . .
I would like a single room.	Enreed hujra li shakhis wahed.
Double room	Enreed hujra muz-dawij
The hotel	Al-hootell (or) Al-funduq
The manager	Al-moodeer
Inquiries	Ista-lamaat
The porter	Al-bawaab
The waiter	Asuf-raaji
The lounge	Assaala
The dining room	Saalet al-akel
The bedroom	Huj-rat annoum
The key	Al-muftaah
The first floor	Attabic al-awel
The bathroom	Al-hammaam
Call me at . . .	Naadeeni anda . . .
6 o'clock	Assa-a sitta
7 o'clock	Assa-a sab-à
I would like to . . .	Enreed (or) Nebbi . . .
Change my room	En-ghayer huj-rati
I shall be back	Sanar-ja
Late	Muta-akher
Early	Muba-kir
Room No.	Rakkem al-huj-ra
Have you any letters?	Hal-lee-risaayel?
Message	Risaala (or) Mukaalema
For me	Lee-ana
Room	Hujra
Luggage	Haqaayeb (or) Shanaati

Bring the bags	**Jeeb al-haqaayeb.**
I shall leave the hotel	**Nebbi net-rek al-funduq.**
At dawn	**Anda al-fajer**
In the morning	**Fee assabaah**
At noon	**Fee nesf annahaar**
My bill please	**Hesaabi min-fad-lak**

IN A RESTAURANT

The menu	Qaayemat al-akel (or) At-taam
The waiter	Assuf-raaji
May I have	Mumken-ta-teeni
Please	Min-fad-lak
Mineral water	Maya-ma-danya
I should like	Nebbi (or) Enreed
An English dish	Ta-aam englieezi
Libyan	Libee
Italian	Itaalee
French	Fran-saawi
Lunch	Ghadaa
Dinner	Ashaa
Breakfast	Futoor
Traditional dish	Ta-aam taq-leedi
Are you serving	Hal al-ghadaa
Lunch now	Jahiz al-ana
Table for two please	Ta-wala lit-nain min naas min-fadlak
Special dish	Ta-aam khusoosi
The bill please	Al-hisaab min-fadlak (m)
Keep the change	Em-sick al-baaqi
Salt	Melah
Peper	Fil-fill
Oile	Zeit
Vinegar	Khall
Sandwich	Sandwish
Spoon	Kaashik
Fork	Shauka
Knife	Moos (or) Sekeen
Plate	Soonya (s) Suwaani (pl)
Glass	Kubbaya (or) Taasa
May I have	Ateeni min-fadlak

51

May we have	**Ateena min-fadlak**
Some Water	**Shewaya maya**
Nothing more	**La-shai aakhar**
Thank you	**Shukran**
Hot water	**Maya sakh-na**
Cold water	**Maya ber-dà**
Open (command)	**Af-tah**
Close	**Sakker** (or **Agh-fell**)
Come	**Ta-aal (m) Ta-aali (f)**
Go	**Emshi (m & f)**
Call a taxi	**Naadili taaxee**
Where is the . . .	**Wain al . . .**
Telephone	**Talafoon** (or **Al-haatif**)
W.C.	**Beit-arraha** (or) **Al-hammam**
Lift	**Mis-add**
Cafe	**Maq-haa**
Restaurant	**Mat-am**
Have you newspapers?	**Andakum jaraayed?**

TRAVEL

My name is . . .	Ismee . . .
I would like to book for . . .	En-reed neh-jezz lee . . .
London	Lee-lundan
Greece	Lil-younaan
Cairo	Lil-qaahira
Germany	Lee-almaanya
Italy	Lee-itaalya
Japan	Lil-yabaan
Spain	Lee-isbaanya
Tunis	Lee-toonis
Algeria	Lil-jazaayer
Morocco	Lil-magh-reb
Turkey	Lee-tourkya
For tomorrow	Lee-bukraa
For next week	Lee-ass-boo almuq-bal
When does the plane depart?	Amta etsaafer attayera?
When does the plane arrive?	Amta tu-sill attayera?
Tell me the flight number.	Ghool-lee raqam arrih-la.
Is there a bus?	Andakum auto-bees?
The bus is fully booked.	Al-auto-bees mah-jooz.
My telephone number is . . .	Raqam talafooni . . .

53

AT THE AIRPORT

Cairo	El cahira
Alexandria	El Askandaria
International	**Du-waly**
Airport	**Mataar El-cahira**
Cairo International Airport	**Mataar addu-wali**
Alexandria	**Mataar Alexandria**
Vaccination	**Tat-eem**
Certificate	**Shahaada**
Passport	**Jawaaz-safr**
Visa	**Tà-sheera**
Entry	**Du-khool**
Exit	**khu-rooj**
The customs	**Al-jamaaregh**
Suitcase or briefcase	**Shanta** (f)
Handbag	**Shantat-yad**
This is my bag	**Hadi-he shanti**
This is not mine	**Hathe-mush-lee**
How many bags ...	**Kam shanta ...**
... do you have	**... Andak (m) (s)**
One bag	**Shanta waheda**
Two bags	**Shantatain**
Three bags	**Talaata shanaatee**
Please open your bag.	**Min-fad-lak aftah ashanta.**
Have you anything to declare?	**Hal-andak ay-shai ?**
I have nothing to declare.	**Ma-andish-shai.**
I have some gifts.	**Andi ba-ath hadaaya lee shakhseeyan.**
It is already opened.	**Maf-tooh.**
I have	**Andi**
Cigarettes	**Sebaasi** (or) **Seghaayer**
Cigars	**Tus-caani**

54

Perfume	**Ra-waayah**
I have no ...	**Ma-andish**
... Spirits	**Kuhool**
Liqueurs	**Mash-roobaat**
Tobacco	**Dakhaan**
Jewellery	**Jawaaher**
That is all I have.	**Hada ma andi.**
Here is my passport.	**Tafadal jawaaz safari.**
I have lost my passport.	**Waddart jawaaz safari.**
I am from ...	**Ana min ...**
Yugoslavia	**You-ghos-lavia**
China	**Asseen**
U.S.A.	**Amreeca**
U.K.	**Britaanya**

AT THE SEAPORT

Seaport	Meenaa
Ship	Baa-khira (or) Safeena
Ticket	Attath-kira
Boat	Qaareb (or) Filooka
Launch	Laanshya (or) Zaurek-bukhari
Goods	Bathaa-ya
Clearance	Tass-reeh
Export	Tas-deer
Import	Taw-reed
Documents	Mus-tanadaat
Parcels	Turood (pl) Tared (s)
Customs duties	Rusoom al-ghum-regh
Tax free	Ma-fee min addareeba
Warehouse	Al-makh-zan
Paid	Mad-fooa (f) Mad-foo (m)
In cash	Naq-dan
I have completed the necessary procedures.	Amalt al-ij-raa-at allazima.
Israel Boycott office	Mak-tab muqata-at israa-eel
Not on the black-list	Mush-fee al-qaayema-assauda

AT THE OFFICE

Your name please	Ismak min-fathlak (m)
My name is . . .	Ismee . . .
Your last name?	Shenu laq-buk (m)?
Your family name?	Shenu ism al-uss-ra?
What is your address?	Shenu an-waanak?
Place of birth	Makaan al-welaadah
Nationality	Al-jensiya
Marital status	Al-haala al-ij-teemaaiya
Single or married	Aazeb aw mutazawej
Salary required	Arraatib al-matloob
Are you now employed?	Hal-tash-taghel tawa?
Do you speak English?	Hal-tata-kallam inglessi?
Very little	Qaleel jiddan.
What is your education?	Shenu taleemak?
Is it primary?	Hal huwa ib-teedaee?
Preparatory	Ee-daadi
Secondary	Tà-nawi
Have you any degrees?	Hal andak shahadaat ul-ya?
Where were you employed?	Wain kunt tash-taghel?
What is the name of the employer?	Shenu ism saa-heb al-amall?
What is the reason for leaving?	Shenu sabab tar'k al-amall?
For salary reasons	Al-asbaab heya arrateb
I would like to see Mr. . . .	Mumken enshoof essayed . . .
He is not in at the moment.	Huwa mush maw-jood tawa.
He will be here at . . .	Yar-jaah essa-a . . .
Can you come back tomorrow?	Taghder (or) mumken tar-jaah buckra?

AT THE PHARMACY

Where is the nearest pharmacy/chemist?	Wain ag-rab saida-liya?
What time does it open?	Saa-a kam taf-tah?
I need some medicines.	Nebbi baa-th al-ad-wiya.
Here is the prescription.	Hathi-he was-fat attabeeb.
Is there a doctor?	Andakum ductoor? (or) Tabeeb.
Yes, there is one in this street.	Ay-wa fee waahad fee hatha ashaara.
Call an ambulance.	Naadi sayarat al-is-aaf.
I have a pain here.	Andi waja (or) Alam hana.
I do not sleep well.	Manar qedish kuwais.
I cannot eat — I have no appetite.	Manaq-darsh na-kul, ma-indish shaheya.
Head	Raa-ss
Eye (s)	Ai-n (s) (Ayoun pl)
Ear (s)	Uthun (s) (Athaan pl)
Mouth	Famm
Tongue	Lisaan
Throat, Sore throat	Hanjara
Arm	The-raa
Hand(s)	Yadd (s) (Yadein pl)
Stomach	Bat-n (or) Ma-eeda

HUMAN RELATIONS

Father	Al-abb
Mother	Al-umm
Boy	Al-walad
Girl	Al-Bint
Children	Al-aw-laad
Child	Al-walad
Brother	Al-akh
Sister	Al-ukh-t
Daughter (s)	Al-bint (s) — Banaat (pl)
Husband	Zaw-j
Wife	Zaw-ja
Sweetheart	Habeeba
Lady (ladies)	Sitt (s) — Sittaat (pl)
Uncle (paternal)	Al-amm
Aunt (paternal)	Al-ammah
Uncle (maternal)	Khaal
Aunt (maternal)	Khaala
Father-in-law	Al-amm
Mother-in-law	Al-ammah
Niece	Ib-net al-akh (m)
	Ib-net al-ukht (f)
Nephew	Iben-al-akh (m)
	Iben-al-ukh-t (f)
Grandmother	Jadda
Grandfather	Jadd

AT A GARAGE

Can you please see my car?

Mum-ken min-fad-lak
t-shoof sayarrati?

I need some repairs to be
done to it.

Nebbi (or) Enreed ba-ath
attas-leehaat lil-
sayaara.

I had a car accident.

Hassal-lee haadith.

Here is the Police authority
to repair the car.

Hatha ithin ashur-tà
li-tas-leeh assayaara.

How much do you want to
do the job?

Kam t-reed (or) Tebbi
li-tà-mal ashooghul?

I need the car as soon as
possible.

Muh-taaj ila assayaara fee
as-rà waqt mum-ken.

May I have it next week?

Mumken na-khuth assay-
aara fee al-is-boo ajja-
ee?

In the mean time please see
the (water for) battery.

Fee nafs-al-waq-t min-
fad-lak shoof-lee
(mayat-) al-battariya.

TO RENT A FLAT

I need a flat to rent.	Muh-taaj ila shuqqa or Shighgha lil-eejaar.
My family will be in Tripoli next month.	Aa-ilati (or) Usra-ti sata-kun fee Trabls ash-shar ajadeed.
Therefore	Litha-lika
The flat must be ready.	Ashuqqa yajib an-takun ja-hiza.
Before my family	Ghabl aa-ilati (or) Usra-ti
The room is small.	Al-hujra sagheera.
The window is big.	Arraw-shan kabeer.
When can we go to see the Other house ?	Amta nagh-dar nemshoo beish enshoofu al-man-zil al-akher ?
I do not work tomorrow.	Manekh-demish buk-ra.
I want to visit the other flat.	Enreed enzoor ashu-ghgha al-ukh-ra.
This appartment is for rent.	Hathi ashuqqa lil-eejaar.
How much is its rent?	Kam eejaar-ha ?
Let us see the . . .	Khaleena enshoof . . .
Cellar	Al-makh-zan
Roof	Assatah
Ground floor	Addour-al-arthe
Wall (s)	Assaas (s) (Seasaan) (pl)
Door (s)	Al-baab (s) (Be-baan) (pl)
Room (s)	Al-hu-j-ra (s) (Hujuraat) (pl)
Ceiling	Assaqaf

Dining-room	**Hu-j-rat al-akel**
Bed-room	**Hu-j-rat annoum**
Bath-room	**Al-hammam**
The Kitchen	**Al-mat-bakh**
The bell	**Ajja-ras**
The street	**Ashaarah**

THE ADMINISTRATION OF EGYPT

Governor	**Muhaafith**
Governorate of Cairo	Muhaafathat El Cahira
Alexandria	El Askandaria
Aswan	Aswan
Luxor	Luxor
Asyout	Asyout
El Menia	El Menia
El Behera	El Behera
El Gharbia	El Gharbia

HOLIDAYS SCHEDULE

The Grand Bayraam	**10, 11 Thul hijja**
The Islamic Year (**HEJRA**)	**1 Muharram**
Ashura	**10 Muharram**
Prophet's Birthday	**12 Rabee awal**
(See Islamic month)	**26 Rajab**
(See Islamic month)	**14 Shaban**
The Lesser Bayraam	**1, 2 Shawal**

VOCABULARY

A

Able	**Qaader**
Aboard the ship	**Ala-assafeena**
About	**An**
Above	**Ala** (or) **Foagh**
Abroad	**Fi-al-khaarij**
Absent	**Ghaaib**
Accept	**Yaq-bel**
Access	**Dukhool**
Accident	**Haadith**
Accommodation	**Istiraaha**
Accompany	**Youraafiq**
Agency	**Wakaala**
Alley	**Zuqaq** (or) **Zangha**
Apartment	**Shuqqa**
Apology	**Eti-thaar**
Appointment	**Mi-aad**
Agenda	**Ber-naamij** (or) **Jad-wal**
Again	**Min-jadeed**
Against	**Thadd**
Age	**Omer** (or) **Senn**
Air	**Hawaa**
Aircraft	**Taa-ira**
Airfield	**Mataar**
Alcohol	**Kuhool**
Alike	**Mutashaabeh**
Alive	**Haee**
All	**Kull**
Alone	**Mun-farid**
Also	**Ai-than**
Ambulance	**Sayaarat al-is-aaf**

Ancient	Qadeem
Anew	Min-jadeed
Angel	Malaak
Anger	Ghadab (or) Za-al
Angry	Za-laan
Animal	Hai-waan
Announcement	Elaan
Annual	Sanawi
Annually	Kul-sanà (or) Sanawi-yan
Answer	Jawaab
Ant	Nam-la
Any	Ay
Anybody	Ay-insaan
Anyhow — Anyway	Ala-kulli-haal
Anyone	Ay-shakh-s
Anyplace — anywhere	Fee ay makaan
Anything	Ay-shai
Apologize	Yà-tathir
Appetite	Sha-hiya
Applause	Tass-feeq
Apple	Tefaaha
Appointment	Ta-een
Appreciate	Youqaddir
Approve	Youwafiq
Approximately	Tak-reeban
Argue	Youjaadel
Argument	Munaaqasha
Arrange	Youratib
Arrangement	Tarteeb
Arrest	Yà-taqel
Arrival	Qoodoom (or) Wosool
Arrive	Yasil
Ashore	Ala-ashaati
Ashtray	Manfa-that saja-eer

Ask	Yat-lub
Asleep	Naayem
Assembly	Jam-eeya
Assure	You-akid
Astonishing	Mud-hish
Atom	Tharra
Aware	Mud-rik
Away	Baeedan
Awful	Mukheef
Axe	Faas

B

Baby	Tefell (m) Tef-la (f)
Bachelor	Aazib
Back	Waraa
Bad	Kabeh
Bag	Haqeeba (or) Shanta
Baggage	Haqaaib (or) Shanaati
Balcony	Shir-fah
Ball	Koora
Bank	Mas-raf
Bathe (v)	Yagh-sil
Bebore	Min-qabil
Beforehand	Mukaddaman
Beg	Yatawassal
Begin	Yab-da
Behind	Khalf
Believe	Yousadiq
Bell	Jaras
Belong	Yakhuss
Belongings	Am-tee-a
Below	Teht
Belt	Hizaam
Bench	Maq-ad
Beneficial	Mufeed
Beside	Be-jaaneb
Best	Al-ah-san
Betray (v)	Yakhoon
Bag	Shanta
Baggage	Amti-à
Bananas	Mouz
Basket	Sella
Bath	Hammam

Beautiful	**Jameel**
Bed	**Sareer**
Bedding	**Fraash**
Between	**Bain** (or) **Ma-bain**
Beware	**Ah-taris**
Big	**Kabeer**
Bill (invoice)	**Fatoura**
Bird (s)	**Tair**
Black	**Aswad**
Blame	**Yaloom**
Bless (v)	**Youbaarik**
Blind (n)	**Mak-foof**
Blood	**Damm**
Blood test (n)	**Fahas-damm**
Blow (v)	**Yanfukh**
Blown	**Manfookh**
Blue	**Az-ragh**
Body	**Jesem**
Book	**Kitaab**
Boot	**Hithaa** (or) **Jaz-ma**
Box	**Sandoogh**
Box office	**Shoobaak attathaker**
Boy friend	**Sadeeq**
Boy scout	**Kashaaf**
Brave	**Shoojaa**
Bread	**Khubza**
Breakfast	**Futoor**
Bring	**Jeeb**
Broken	**Mak-soor**
Brown	**As-mar**
Buy	**Yash-tiri**
Beside	**Be-jaaneb**

Beverage	**Mash-roob**
Bill	**Fatoura**
Boat	**Markep**
Burglary	**Satù (or) Sergha**
Butcher	**Jazzaar**

Cabbage	Karanb
Cabdriver	Saayeq sayaara
Cabin	Hujra (or) Ghabina
Cable	Bar-qeya
Café (place)	Maq-hà
Cage	Qafas
Camera	Aalet-tass-wir
Camp	Mukhayem
Cancel	Yash-teb
Cancellation	Shataba
Candle	Sham-aa
Candlestick	Sham-aadaan
Carpet	Sajaada
Cart	Karroosa
Cash	Naqad (filoos)
Catch (v)	Yam-sik
Cause (n)	Sabab
Celebrate (v)	Yah-tafell
Celebration	Ih-tifaal
Center	Wasat
Certification	Shahaadah
Chain (n)	Sil-sila
Chair	Kursee
Chalk	Tabasheer
Change (v)	You-ghayer
Charming (n)	Faatin (or) Jameel
Chart	Khareeta
Chicken	Dajaaja
Child	Tefil
Church	Kaneesa
Circumcision	Khitaan (or) Tahaara
Civil	Mutamaddin

Civilian	**Madani**
Civilization	**Al-madaniya**
Clean	**Natheef**
Clear	**Saafee**
Clerk	**Kaatib** (or) **Muathaf**
Clever	**Thakee**
Client (customer)	**Zaboon**
Clinic	**Eeyada**
Clock	**Saa-a**
Cloth	**Ghamaash**
Clothes	**Malaabis**
Cloud	**Sahaaba**
Coal	**Fihem**
Coast	**Saahell**
Cock	**Deek**
Coffee	**Ghah-wa**
Coffee house	**Ghah-wa**
Cold	**Baarid**
Colour	**Loan**
Come	**Ta-aal**
Common (general)	**Umoomi**
Compartment	**Huj-ra**
Cable	**Barqiya**
Capital	**Aasima**
Car	**Sayyara**
Cashier	**Sarraf**
Certificate	**Shahaada** (or) **Wateeka**
Chemist	**Saydali**
Church	**Keneesa**
Clinic	**Mustawsif**
Clothes	**Malaabis**
Coast	**Saahel al-bahar**
Coffee	**Ghah-wa**
Complaint	**Shak-wa**

71

Congratulations	Mab-rook
Consul	Ghansol
Conversation	Hadeeth
Conveyance	Nakel
Cosmetics	Adawaat azeena

D

Dam	**Khazaan**
Damp	**Ratab'**
Dance	**Reghas**
Daughter	**Ibna**
Deliver	**Sallama**
Dentist	**Tabeeb asnaan**
Deodorizer	**Muzeell arra-iha**
Depart	**Safara (or) Rahala**
Deposit	**Magh-zan**
Desert	**Sah-ra**
Dessert	**Faakiha**
Destination	**Jihat al-Oosool**
Dine	**Ta-asha**
Dinner	**Ashaa**
Direction	**Jeehaa**
District	**Muqaata-a**
Doctor	**Tabeeb**
Document	**Mustanid**
Door	**Baab**
Dress	**Eustaan**
Driver	**Sawaagh**

E

Each	**Kul-waahed**
Eager	**Muta-hammis**
Ear (s)	**Uthen (s) athaan (pl)**
Early	**Bak-ree**
Earn — earning	**Yak-sab**
East	**Sharq**
Easy	**Saahel**
Eat	**Yakul**
Egg (s)	**Baitha (s) bayth (pl) (or)**
Elastic	**Mataat**
Elbow	**Mirfaq**
Electric — electricity	**Kah-raba**
Elevator	**Mis-aad**
Emergency	**Musta-jil**
Employee	**Mua-daf**
Empty	**Faaragh**
End	**Nihaaya**
Enjoy	**Yatamatà**
Enter	**Yad-khul**
Entire	**Jamee**
Entrance	**Dukhool**
Envelope (s)	**Tharef (s) thuroof (pl)**
Equal	**Musaawi**
Equipment	**Mu-a-ddaat**
Error	**Khataa**
Essential	**Thuroori**
Even	**Hatta**
Evening	**Layl (or) Lail**
Every	**Kul**
Everything	**Kul-shay**
Everywhere	**Fe-kul-makaan**
Except	**Illa (or) ma-ada**

Excuse	Iti-daar
Expect	Yatawaqa
Expensive	Ghaali
Explain	Youfassir
Explanation	Taf-seer
Expression	Ta-beer
Extra	Zi-yada
Eye (s)	Ain (s) ayoun (pl)
Eyebrow (s)	Hajib al-ain (s) hawaajib (pl)
Eyelash (es)	Rumoosh

F

Fabric	Naseej
Face	Wajah
Fact (s)	Haqeeqa (s) haqaa-iq (pl)
Faint	Baa-hit
Fair	Aadel
Fall — falling	Saqata
False	Zaaif
Familiar	Aadee
Family	Us-ra
Far	Baeed
Farm	Maz-ra-a
Farther	Ab-ad
Fast	Saree
Fat	Sameen
Father	Ab
February	Feb-raayer
Feel — feeling	Yash-ur
Female	Mu-annat
Few	Qaleel
Field (s)	Haqal (s) huqool (pl)
Fifth	Khaams
Fig	Teen
Fill	Yamla
Film	Film
Find	Yajid
Fine	Kuways
Finger (s)	Saba (s) asaaba (pl)
Finish	Yantahi

Finished	Antaha
Fire	Naar (or) hareegha
First	Awal
Fish	Samak (or) hoot
Floor	Taabeq
Flour	Degheegh
Flower (s)	Zah-ra (s) zuhoor (pl)
Follow	Yat-bà
Food	Akel (or) ta-am
Foot — feet	Kadam (s) akdaam (pl)
Football	Kurat kadam
For	Lee
Foreigner	Aj-nabi
Forget	Nasaa
Fork (s)	Shouka (s) shuwak (pl)
Found	Wajada
Fourth	Raaba
Frame (s)	Burwaaz (s) barawiz (pl)
Free	Hurr
Frequent	Mutakarir
Fresh	Taaza
Friday	Youm ajjuma
Friend (s)	Sadeeq (s) asdiqaa (pl)
From	Min
Front	Amaam
Fruit	Faakiha
Full	Mal-aan (or) mal-yaan
Fun	Mazaah
Funny	Muth-hik
Fur	Faroo

Furniture	Ataat
Further	Aithan
Fuss	Daw sha
Future	Mustak-bel

G

Game	Yal-ab
Garage	Gharaaj
Garden	Hadeeqa (or) saanya
Garlic	Thoom
Gas	Ghaaz
General	Umoomi
Generous	Kareem
Girl (s)	Bint (s) banaat (pl)
Give	Ya-tee
Glad	Farhaan
Glass (es)	Zujaaj (natharaat)
Glove	Qafaaz
Go — going	Yamshi
Goat	Mà-za
Gold	Thahab
Gone	Mashaa
Good	Kuways
Grape	Anab
Grass	Hasheesh
Grateful	Mutashaker
Green	Akh-thar
Grey	Ramaadi
Guess	Takh-meen
Guest	Thaif
Guide	Mur-shid

H

Had	Kaan anda
Hair	Sha-ar
Half	Nesf
Hallo	Ah-lan
Hammer	Ghadoom
Hand (s)	Yad (s) yadain (pl)
Handbag	Shantat-yad
Happen	Yah-deth
Happy	Saeed
Hard	Sa-ab
Hat	Taghiya
Have	Anda
He	Huwa
Head	Raas
Health — healthy	Seh-ha
Hear	Yas-ma
Heart	Qalb (or) ghalb
Heat	Haraara
Heavy	Tigheel
Heel	Ka-ab
Height	Tool (col) irtifah (clas)
Help	Yousaad
Hen	Dajaaja
Here	Hunà (or) Hanà
Hers	Laha
Herself	Eb-nafsaha
Hide	Ediss
High	Aalee
Hill	Ul-wa
His	Lahu
Hold	Yemsik
Hole	Hufra

Holiday	Ot-lah
Home	Manzil
Honest	Sherif
Honey	Asall
Hope	Amal
Horse	Hesaan
Hose	Khartoom
Hospital	Mustash-fa
Hot	Saakhen (or) haar
Hour	Saa-a
House	Housh (or) manzil
How	Keif
Huge	Kabeer
Humour — humourous	Tas-liya — musally (adj)
Hunger –– hungry	Ja-aan (adj)
Hurry up	Es-raa (clas) feesah (colq)
Hurt	E-wajah
Husband	Zouj

I	Ana
Ice	Thelej (or) Tilij
Idea	Fikra
Idle	Kas-laan
If	Low
Ill	Mareeth
Illegal	Ghair qanoony
Imagination	Khayaal
Imitation	Taq-leed
Immediate — immediately	Saree — be-sur-a
Impatient	Mush saboor
Import (s)	Eewarrid (v) waaridaat (n)
Important	Muhem
Improve — improvement	You-hassen (v) tah-seen (n)
In	Fee
Incapable	Aajiz
Inch	Bousah
Include — including	Youd-khel (v) yesh-mal
Inconvenient	Mush munaaseb
Incorrect	Ghalat
Increase	Eezeed (or) zaada (v)
Indeed	Fe-lan (or) ha-qan
Indefinite	Mush-maroof
Indicate	Eesheer ila
Indication	Eshaarah
Individual	Shakh-si
Infection	Talaweth
Ink	Hebar
Inside	Dakhel
Intelligent	Thakey
Interest	Faa-ida

Interesting	Mufeed
Interpret (er)	Tar-jum — tarjooman
Introduce	You-arif be
Invite	Yad-oo
Invitation	Dawa
Iron	Hadeed
Is	Yakoon
It	Huwa (m) heya (f)

J

Jacket	**Jakait** (or) **sit-ra**
January	**Yannair**
June	**Youn-you**
Judge	**Qaathee**
Jam	**Iz-dihaam**
Japan	**Al-yabaan**
Jar	**Jarra** (or) **ib-reeq**
Jaw	**Fakk**
Jealous	**Ghayour (naghaar)**
Jewel — jewelry	**Hella** (or) **jawaaher**
Job	**Amal** (or) **shooghel**
Join	**Yarbit**
Joined	**Rabata**
Joke	**Nuk-ta — mazaah**
Journey	**Rih-lah**
Jug — jar	**Ib-reeq**
Juice	**Aseer**
July	**You-liyou**
Jump	**Yaq-fiz**
Junior	**Sagheer**
Justice	**Adaalah**

K

Keep	Yah-fith (v)
Kerosene	Ghaaz
Kettle	Saghaan
Key (s)	Mif-tah (s) mafateeh (pl)
Kick	Yarfis (v)
Kidney	Kil-wa
Kind (adj)	Lateef
Kitchen	Mat-bakh
Kitten	Ghatoos
Knee	Rok-ba
Knife	Moos
Knives	Amuaas
Knock	Yat-roq (or) yaduq (v)
Knot	Oq-da
Know	Ya-rif (v)

L

Ladder	Saloom
Lady — ladies	Sayeda — sayedaat
Lamb (s)	Kharoof — khir-faan
Lamp	Misbaah (or) lamba
Land	Arth
Language	Loogha
Large	Kabeer
Last	Aakhir
Late	Muta-akhir
Laugh	Yath-hak (v)
Laundry	Magh-sila
Law (s)	Qanoon — qawaneen
Lawyer	Muhaami
Leaf	Waraqa (clas) wer-gha (colq)
Lean	Naheef
Learn	Yata-allam (v)
Lease	Eejaar
Least	Al-aqal
Leather	Jeld
Leave	Ejaza
Left	Yesaar
Leg (s)	Saagh (s) seghaan (pl)
Legal	Shar-ee
Lemon (s)	Laymoon (or) leem ghaaris
Lend	Yousalef (v)
Length	Tool
Less	Aaqal
Lesson	Dares

English	Arabic
Letter (s)	Risaala (s) risaayel (pl)
Lettuce	Khass
Level	Mizaan
Library	Mak-taba (or) daar lil-kutub
Licence	Rukh-sa
Lid	Ghitaa
Lie	Kath-ba
Life	Hayaat
Lift	Mis-ad
Light	Thaee
Like	Mithil
Linen	Kettaan
Lip	Shiffa
Liquid	Saayel
List (s)	Qaaima (s) qawaaim (pl)
Little	Shiwaya (or) kaleel
Live — living	Ya-eesh — maeesha
Liver	Kabda
Loaf	Ragheef
Local	Maj-las
Lock (s)	Qifill (s) aq-faal (pl)
Long	Taweel
Look	Enthar (v) (or) shoof
Loose	Mush marboot
Lose	Thaa-a — faqada
Lost	Maf-good
Lot	Koum
Loud	Aali
Lovely	Lateef (or) jameel
Low	Rakhees

Luck	Naseeb (or) bakh-t
Luggage	Am-teea
Lunch	Ghatha (or) ghada
Lung	Ree-a (or) ree-ya

M

Macaroni	Makaroona
Machine	Aalah
Mad	Mah-bool
Magazine	Majalla
Magnificent	Atheem
Maid	Al-khaadima
Mail	Rasaayel
Male	Thakar
Manicure	Tas-wiyat al-athaafer
Many	Katheer (or) wajid (or)
Map	Khareeta
Marriage	Zawaaj
Market	Soogh
Master (Teacher)	Mudarris
Match (es)	Keb-reet (or) ugheed
Material	Adawaat
Meal	Waj-ba
Measure	Miq-yaas
Mechanic	Mekaniki
Medicine	Ad-wiya (or) dawa
Medium	Mutawasit
Meet	Yaj-tami ila
Meeting	Ij-timaa
Melon	Bittekh
Member	Athou
Mend	Yousallah (v)
Mention	Ishaara (or) youthakir (v)
Menu	Qaai-mat attaam
Merchant	Taajir
Merely	Faqat
Message	Risaalah
Messenger	Faraash

Middle	**Wast** (or) **mutawassit**
Mild	**Mutadil** (or) **lateef**
Milk	**Haleeb** (or) **laban**
Mine	**Lee**
Minimum	**Al-had al-adna**
Minister	**Wazir**
Ministry	**Wazaara**
Mint	**Naa-naah**
Minute	**Daqeeqa (digheegha)**
Mirror	**Emraaya**
Miserable	**Mukh-zee** (or) **paees**
Mistake	**Khatah** (or) **ghalat**
Misunderstand	**Soo-tafaahim**
Mix	**Youkhalet (v)**
Model	**Shakel** (or) **tiraaz**
Moderate	**Mutadil**
Modern	**Hadeeth**
Moment	**Lah-tha**
Monday	**Youm al-it-nain**
Money	**Nukood or filoos**
Month	**Shahar**
Moon	**Al-qamar**
More	**Ziyada** (or) **ukhra**
Morning	**Sabaah**
Mosquito	**Namoos** (or) **baootha**
Most	**Al-akthariya**
Mother	**Om**
Mountain	**Jabal**
Mourn	**Hidaad** (or) **hazen**
Mouse	**Faar**
Moustache	**Shanabaat**
Mouth	**Fam**
Move	**Yataharak (v)**
Much	**Wajid**

Mud	Uahel
Muddle	Youkhal-bet
Murder	Jareema
Mushroom	Fa-ghaah
Music	Muzeeka
Must	Yajib
Mutton	Laham kharoof
Mutual	Mush-tarek
My	Lee
Myself	Naf-see
Mysterious	Ghareeb
Mystery	Sirr

Nail (s)	Mas-maar — masaameer
Name (s)	Ism — asmaa
Napkin (s)	Foota — fuwat
Narrow	Thayeq
Nasty	Mush-kuwis
Nationality	Al-jensiya
Natural	Tabee-ee
Near — nearby	Qareeb
Neat	Muratib
Necessary	Thuroory
Neck	Roq-ba
Necklace	Qilaada
Need	Yah-taaj
Needle (s)	Ib-ra — eebaari
Neighbour (s)	Jaar — jiraan
Never	Abadan
New	Jadeed
News	Akh-baar
Newspaper	Jareeda
Next	Attaali
Nice	Kuways
Night	Layl (or) lail
Nine	Tis-aa
No	La
Noise — noisy	Dou-sha
None	La-shay
Noon	Thuhur
No-one	Wala wahed
Nor	La
Normal	Tabee-ee
North	Shimaal
Nothing	La-shay

Nose	**Anf**
Not	**La**
Note	**Muthakira**
Notice	**Eelaan**
Novel	**Riwaya (or) qissaah**
November	**Noovember**
Now	**Tawa (or) al-aan**
Nowhere	**Wa-la-makaan**
Nuisance	**Iz-aaj**
Number (s)	**Raqem (s) arqaam (pl)**
Nurse	**Mumaritha**
Nursery	**Al-hathaana**
Nut	**Louz**
Nylon	**Nai-lon**

O

Obedient — obedience	**Muteè**
Object	**Shay**
Oblige — obligation	**Wajib**
Observe	**Laahith** (or) **shoof**
Obstinate	**Aneed**
Obtain	**Yatahasil**
Occasion	**Munaasiba**
Occupation	**Watheefa**
Occur	**Hadatha** (v)
October	**Octouber**
Odd	**Muf-rad**
Of	**Emta**
Offence	**Eehaana**
Offend	**Youthayeq**
Offer	**Youkadem**
Office	**Mak-tab**
Officer	**Thaabit**
Often	**Ghaaliban**
Oil	**Zeit**
Ointment	**Bumaata** (or) **dehaan**
Old	**Kabeer**
Olive	**Zeitoon**
On	**Ala**
Once	**Marra**
One	**Wahed**
Onion	**Basal**
Only	**Bass**
Onward	**Laghiddaam**
Open	**Yaf-tah** (v)
Opinion	**Raay** (or) **fikra**
Opportunity	**Fursa**
Opposite	**Ax**

Optician	**Natharaati**
Optimism	**Tafaawel**
Or	**Aw**
Orange	**Berteghaal**
Orchestra	**Firqa muzeekeya**
Ordinary	**Aadee**
Organize	**Younathim**
Origin	**Asel**
Ornament	**Zeena**
Orphan — orphanage	**Yateem — mal-ja**
Other	**Akher**
Otherwise	**Wa-illa**
Our (s)	**Emta-na**
Ourselves	**En-fus-na**
Out	**Barra (or) khaarij**
Outside	**Khaarij**
Oven	**Furen (or) koosha**
Over	**Ala**
Owner	**Maalik**

Package	**Ghertaas**
Padlock	**Ghefell**
Page	**Saf-ha**
Paid	**Khaales**
Pain	**Alam** (or) **waja**
Paint — painter	**Dihan**
Paintbrush	**Furshah**
Paintings	**Rusoomaat**
Pair	**Zouj**
Pale	**Shahab**
Palm	**Kaff**
Panic	**Mukheef**
Paper	**Waragha**
Paragraph	**Faqara**
Parcel	**Tared**
Parliament	**Maj-lis al-umma**
Part	**Juz-oo**
Partial	**Mutahaiz**
Participant	**Mush-tarik**
Particular	**Khusoosi**
Partner	**Shareek**
Party	**Haf-la**
Passage	**Mamarr**
Passenger	**Raakib** (or) **musaafir**
Passport	**Jawaaz-safar**
Past	**Maathee**
Patient	**Mareeth**

Patriot	Watani
Pavement	Arthiya
Pay	Yad-fa
Payment	Dafaa
Peace	Salaam
Peach	Khookh
Peanut	Fool sudani
Pear	Kometra
Peculiar	Ghareeb
Pedestrian	Mushaat
Peg	Mis-jab
Pen	Ghalam
Penalty	Jazaa
Pencil	Ghalam rasaas
People	Sha-ab (or) naas
Pepper	Fil-fil
Perfect	Kaamel
Perform	Younjiz (v)
Perfume	Raaiha (or) otoor
Perhaps	Rubbama
Permit — permission	Yasmah (v) ithin
Person	Shakh-s
Persuade	Yaq-na (v)
Petrol	Naf-ta
Pharmacy	Sai-daliya
Photograph	Soora
Physician	Tabeeb
Piano	Aalet al-bianu
Picnic	Nuzha

Picture (s)	Soora
Piece (s)	Qit-aa — qitaa
Pigeon (s)	Hamaama — hamaam
Pilgrim --- Pilgrimage	Al-haj — yahej
Pill (s)	Huboob
Pilot (s)	Rabban attayara
Pin (s)	Daboos — dabaabees
Pink	Gharenfel
Pity	Yakh-saara
Place	Makaan
Plain	Baseet
Plant (s)	Shajara — shajar
Plastic	Plastic
Please	Min-fath-lak
Plenty	Wajid
Pocket (s)	Jaib — jiyoub
Poison	Sim
Police	Shurti
Politics -- politician	Sayasa — seyasi
Poor	Faqeer
Popular	Ma-roof
Port	Meena
Porter	Hammaal (or) bawaab
Position	Makaan
Possible	Mumken
Postage stamp	Taaba bareed
Postcard	Kartoolina
Post office	Al-bareed
Potato (es)	Bataatas

98

Poultry	**Addajaaj**
Practical	**Amali**
Practise	**Yatadarrab**
Precious	**Tameen**
Prefer	**Youfathel (v)**
Prepare	**Youjahiz (v)**
Prescribe	**Yousaf (v)**
Prescription	**Wasfa**
Present	**Maujood**
President	**Raees**
Pretty	**Jameel**
Previous	**Min-qabel**
Prison	**Sejin**
Private	**Khusoosi**
Prize	**Jaiza**
Probably	**Mumken**
Procedure	**Tareeqa**
Program	**Jad-wal**
Progress	**Yataqaddam**
Promise	**Wa-ad**
Prompt	**Aajil**
Proper	**Munaasib**
Protect	**Yah-me (v)**
Prove	**Youbarhin (v)**
Proverb	**Matall**
Provide	**Youzawid (v)**
Pulse	**Nabeth**
Pump	**Yanfikh (v)**
Punctual	**Fee al-mi-aad**

Puncture	Taqab
Pupil	Til-meeth
Purchase	Yashtari (v)
Pure	Saafi
Purse	Shanta

Q

Qualification (s)	**Mua-hal (s) mua-halaat (pl)**
Quality	**Shakel**
Quantity	**Miq-daar**
Quarter	**Ruba**
Question	**Soo-aal**
Queue	**Taboor**
Quick	**Saree**
Quiet	**Hudoo**
Quit	**Yat-rok (v)**
Quote	**Yousheer (v)**

R

Rabbit (s)	Ar-nab — araanib
Radio	Radiu
Rain	Matar
Raisin (s)	Zebeeb
Ran	Yaj-ri (v)
Rare	Naadir
Raspberry	Ef-rawla
Rather	Bil-akhass
Reach	Yasel ila (v)
Read	Yaq-ra (v)
Ready	Jaahiz
Real	Haqeeqi
Reason	Sabab
Receipt	Eesaal
Receive	Yastalim (v)
Recognize	Yata-araf (v)
Recipe	Wasfa tabbiya
Red	Ah-mar
Refrigerator	Tallaja
Refuse	Yar-futh (v)
Regret	Muta-assif
Regular	Aadi
Relation	Qaraaba
Relax	Yastareeh
Religion	Deen
Reluctant	Mu-aarith
Remainder	Baqee
Remark	Mulaahtha
Remedy	Eelaaj
Remember	Yatathakar (v)

Rent	**Eejaar**
Repeat	**Youkarir (v)**
Replace	**Youstabdil (v)**
Reply	**Youjeeb (v)**
Represent	**Youmatil (v)**
Representative	**Tamteel**
Require	**Yah-taaj (v)**
Resign	**Yas-taqeel (v)**
Respect	**Yah-tarem (v)**
Responsible	**Mas-ool**
Restaurant	**Mat-am**
Result	**Nateeja**
Return	**Ya-ood (v)**
Reward	**Mukaafa-a**
Rice	**Rez**
Rich	**Ghanee**
Ride	**Yarkab (v)**
Ridiculous	**Sakheef**
Right	**Saheeh**
Rigid	**Shadeed**
Ring	**Khaatim**
Ripe	**Naathij**
Risk	**Youjazif (v)**
River	**Naher**
Road	**Tareegh**
Roast	**Mash-wi**
Rock (s)	**Sakh-ra — sukhoor**
Roof	**Saqaf**
Room	**Huj-ra**
Rope	**Habel**
Rose	**Warda**
Round	**Mustadeer**

Ruin	Kharaab
Ruler	Haakem
Run — running	Yaj-ri (v)
Russian	Rusee

Sack	Esh-waal
Sad	Hazeen
Safe	Saalem
Salad	Salaata
Salary	Raatib
Sale	Yabee (v)
Salt	Melah
Same	Naf-ashay
Sand	Ramel
Satisfy	Yar-tha (v)
Satisfaction	Ratha
Saturday	Youm-assabt
Saucer	Fenjaan
Scarce	Naadir
Scent	Yashim (v)
Schedule	Bir-naamij
Scissor	Maqass
Scorpion	Agh-rab
Sea	Bahar
Search	Efatish (v)
Season	Fasel
Seat	Magh-ad
Second	Attani
Secret	Sirr
See	Yanthur (v) (or) shoof
Seldom	Nadir
Select	Yakh-taar (v)

Sell	Yabee (v)
Send	Yar-sul (v)
Senior	Ra-ees
Sensible	Hassaas
Sentence	Jumla
Separate	Yaf-rez (v)
September	Seb-tember
Serve	Yakh-dum
Service	Khad-ma
Several	Katheer
Severe	Shadeed
Sew	Youkhayet (v)
Shade	Thall
Shake	Yahizz (v)
Shape	Shakel
Shave	Yah-leq (v)
She	Heya
Sheep	Ghanam
Sheet (s)	Warqa (s) awraagh (pl)
Shelf	Raff
Shine	Yal-ma (v)
Ship	Safeena
Shirt (s)	Qamees — qam-saan
Shoe (s)	Kin-dara — kinaader
Shop (s)	Dekkan — dakaakin
Short	Qaseer
Shut	Yaq-fell
Sick	Mareeth
Sight	Mash-had
Sign	Eshaara

Signature	**Taw-qeea**
Silence — silent	**Sukoot — saaket**
Silk	**Hareer**
Silver	**Fathaa**
Similar	**Mutashaabih**
Simple	**Baseet**
Since	**Munthu**
Sincere	**Sareeh**
Sing	**Youghanni (v)**
Single	**Muf-rad**
Sir	**Sayed**
Sister	**Ukh-t**
Sit	**Yaj-lis (v)**
Situation	**Haala**
Size	**Hejim**
Skin	**Jild**
Skirt	**Tanoora**
Sky	**Samaa**
Slang	**Lugha daarija**
Sleep	**Yanaam (v)**
Slow	**Batee**
Small	**Sagheer**
Smell	**Yashim (v)**
Smile	**Yab-tasim (v)**
Smoke	**Dakhaan**
Snake	**Thuaban**
So	**Hakatha**
Soap	**Saboon**
Sofa	**Saloan**
Soft	**Naa-em**

Soil	Taw-qesa
Soldier	Sukoor — snaker
Solicitor	Harter
Solution	Fatbsa
Some	Muteahaqah
Something	Besser
Sometimes	Muntiu
Somewhere	Sareeh
Son	Youghanni (v)
Song	Mut-rad
Soon	Sayed
Sorry	Ukh-t
Soup	Yajils (v)
South	Hsala
Space	Hajim
Speak	Jlld
Special	Tandora
Speech	Samea mos
Speed	Lvgha deerijs
Spend	Yanaam (v)
Spinach	Batee
Sponge	Saphear
Spoon (s)	Yastim (v)
Sport	Yeb-tsaim (v)
Spring	Daldhan
Square	Thunban
Stand	nakartha
Star (s)	Saneen
Start	Saieez
Stay	Yas-em

Soil	Taw-qesa	You – wasikh (v)
Soldier		As-keri (or) jundi
Solicitor		Muhaami
Solution		Hell
Some		Baath
Something		Baath-ashay
Sometimes		Ah-yaanan
Somewhere		Fee-makanin-ma
Son		Ibin
Song		Ugh-niya
Soon		Qareeban
Sorry		Aasif
Soup		Sharba
South		Junoob
Space		Makaan
Speak		Yatakallam
Special		Khusoosi
Speech		Khitaab
Speed		Sur-aa
Spend		Yas-ref (v)
Spinach		Esbanaaq
Sponge		Esfenja
Spoon (s)		Mal-aka
Sport		Ree-yada
Spring		Rabee
Square		Meedan
Stand		Yaqif (v)
Star (s)		Najim — nujoom
Start		Yab-da (v)
Stay		Yata-waqif (v)

Steady	**Taabit**
Steal	**Yas-rugh (v)**
Steam	**Bukhaar**
Step (s)	**Daraja — durooj**
Still	**Ma-zaal**
Stomach	**Maa-ida**
Stop	**Yata-waqif (v)**
Storm	**Aasifa**
Story	**Hakaya**
Strange	**Ghareeb**
Street	**Shara**
Strict	**Qaasee**
String	**Khaet**
Strong	**Qawi**
Stubborn	**Aneed**
Study	**Yad-rus (v)**
Stupid	**Ghabee**
Subject	**Maw-thoo**
Submit	**You-qadim (v)**
Success	**Najaah**
Such	**Matell**
Suddenly	**Fuj-atan**
Sufficient	**Kaafi**
Sugar	**Sukker**
Suggestion	**Eq-tiraah**
Summer	**Seif**
Sun	**Ashams**
Sunday	**Youm-al-ahad**
Sunglasses	**Em-rayaat**
Suppose	**Li-naf-rith**

Sure	Muta-akid
Surgeon	Jaraah
Surname	Ism al-usra
Suspicious	Mureeb
Swim	Ya-oom

T

Table	**Taw-la**
Tailor	**Taarzi**
Take	**Yakhuth (v)**
Talcum powder	**Bood-ra**
Talk	**Yatakallam (v)**
Tall	**Tawil**
Tax — taxes	**Thareeba — tharaaib**
Taxi	**Sayyaarat — uj-ra (taxi)**
Tea	**Shaa-ee**
Teach	**You-allim (v)**
Teeth	**As-naan**
Telegram	**Barqiya**
Telephone	**Haatif**
Television	**Etha-aa mar-eeya**
Tenant	**Al-mus-ta-jir**
Thank	**Shuk-ran**
The	**Al**
Then	**Ba-dain**
There	**Hanaak**
Therefore	**Wa-li-thalika**
Thermometer	**Ter-momiter**
Thick	**Sameek**
Thin	**Rafee**
Thing	**Shay**
Think	**Youfakir (v)**
Third	**Thaalith**
Throat	**Henjara**
Through	**Khilaal**
Thumb	**Ib-haam**
Thunder	**Ra-ad**
Thursday	**Youm-al-khamis**
Ticket	**Tath-kira**

111

Timber	Khashab
Time	Wagh-t
Tin	Safeeha
Tired	Ta-baan
To	Ila
Tobacco	Dakhaan
Today	Al-youm
Together	Ma-an
Tongue	Lisaan
Too	Ai-than
Tools	Adawaat
Touch	Yal-mas (v)
Tough	Hazim
Tourist (s)	Saayah — soowaah
Toward	Ila
Towel (s)	Manshif — manaashif
Town	Madeena
Toy (s)	La-baa — al-aab
Traffic	Harakat-al-muroor
Translate	Youtarjim (v)
Transport	Yan-qul (v)
Travel	Yousaafir (v)
Trouble	Mush-kila
Trousers	Sar-waal — saraweel
Try — trying	You-jarrib (v)
Tuesday	Youm-attelaat
Typist	Tabbaa

U

Ugly	Khabih
Umbrella	Shamsiya
Under	Tehit
Understand	Yaf-ham (v)
Union	Ittihaad
Until	Hatta
Up — upon	Ala
Use — used	Yas-tamel (v)

V

Vacation	**Ejaaza**
Valuable	**Tameen**
Variety	**Tash-keela**
Various	**Mutana-wa**
Vase	**Zuh-riya**
Vegetable	**Khuth-rawaat**
Vehicle	**Sayyaara**
Verify	**You-akid (v)**
Vernacular	**Baladee**
Versatile	**Mutaqalib**
Very	**Jiddan**
View	**Manthar**
Village	**Qariya**
Vinegar	**Khall**
Visa	**Ta-shira**
Visit	**Yazoor (v)**
Visitor	**Zaayer**
Vocabulary	**Muf-raadaat**
Voice	**Sout**

W

Wage	Maa-hiya
Wait	Yantather (v)
Waiter	Saf-raaji
Walk	Yamshi (v)
Want	Yah-taaj (v)
Warm	Daafi
Wash	Yagh-sul (v)
Watch	Yas-har (v)
Water	Em-maya
Water melon	Battikha
Way	Tareegh
We	Nah-nu
Week	Es-boo
Welcome	Mar-haba
West	Gharb
Wet	Mab-lool
What	Matha ?
Whatever	Mah-ma yakoon
Wheel	Aj-laa
When?	Mata
Where?	Aina ?
Which?	Ai ?
While	Bai-nama
White	Ab-yath
Who?	Man ?
Whole	Kull
Why?	Limatha
Wide	Waasa
Wife	Zaw-Ja
Wind	Reeh
Window	Row-shan
Winter	Shitaa

Wish	Yarghab (v)
With	Ma-a
Without	Be-doon
Woman — women	Mar-à — nis-waan
Wool	Soof
Word (s)	Kalime — kalimaat
Work	Shughul
World	Addunya (or) al-aalem
Worse	As-wa
Wrist	Mi-sam
Write	Yak-tub (v)
Wrong	Ghalat

Y

Yard	**Finaa**
Yawn	**Yatataweb (v)**
Year	**Sana (or) aam**
Yellow	**As-far**
Yesterday	**Ams**
Yes	**Aywa (or) na-am**
Yet	**Ma-zaal**
Young	**Sagheer**
Youth	**Shaab**

Z

Zebra	**Himaar wahish**
Zero	**Sifer**
Zinc	**Zinghu**
Zone	**Mantaqa**
Zoo	**Hadeeqat al-haiwanaat**